FRISKY
AND
THE DJ DAYDREAMS

Frisky DJ

Ahem!
The teacher cleared her throat and Frisky suddenly remembered where he was.
"Is this lesson not exciting enough for you?" the teacher asked, raising her eyebrow.
Oh dear, thought Frisky. He really had to stop daydreaming in class.

"Sorry, miss," he said. "It won't happen again."
It was the second time he had been caught staring
into space today and Frisky knew exactly why.
He was daydreaming about listening to the radio on
his walk home from school...

Frisky just couldn't help it!
If he wasn't listening to music and making up his own intros and commentary to songs, then he was daydreaming about it. Every time school got just a little bit boring, then BOOM, he was back to his thoughts.

"Hey, Frisky!" his friend called out, when school was over for the day. "We're going to the park, you want to join?" "I'm OK, thanks," he said, putting on his headphones. "It's the drive-time show. I never miss it."

As he walked through his hometown of Leyton, his little portable radio sticking out of his pocket, Frisky lost himself in a world of beats and rhythm and self-expression.
He loved the music, but his favourite thing by far was pretending he was the DJ himself.

When a song finished, he'd tell his pretend audience why he'd chosen that track and what was coming up next, putting on his best DJ voice. On those walks home, the streets of London were his, and he was Frisky DJ.

It was true, however, that not everyone loved the radio as much as he did...
In fact, there was one kid that always made sure to remind Frisky that he was a little different than everyone else. When he was almost home, Frisky felt a hand on his shoulder.
It was him. Danny.

"Everyone can hear you talking to yourself, Frisky," Danny said. "Why don't you play basketball like us, instead of being weird?" Frisky just shrugged and smiled.
"Because when you're playing basketball," he said to Danny. "I'll be DJing the after party!"

Danny just laughed.

"People round here don't become DJs," he said. "And people don't go to sports games to listen to music. It'll never happen, Frisky."

But Frisky just carried on walking. He'd heard that plenty of times, but nothing was going to stop him enjoying the radio.

When he got back home, he took off his headphones and told his mum about his day.
All through dinner he told her about the new music he'd heard, his favourite lyrics and what he'd been listening to. She smiled. As usual, she had no idea what he was talking about, but she was glad he had found something he liked.

"You know," she said, when she was clearing up the plates, "It's your uncle's birthday party next weekend. Maybe you could sort out the music for it?"
Frisky's eyes lit up. Within a minute he already had a whole load of ideas. This was going to be amazing!

And then things took off.
When his uncle's birthday turned out to be a huge success, Frisky wanted more. He started doing lunchtime sets at school with his Walkman and a tiny speaker, taking requests from his classmates and giving them shoutouts from his playground studio.

Nothing could stop Frisky from following his dream and he carried on doing as many sets, at any kind of party he could right up until he went to high school.
And that's when he took his chance.

He'd heard that his local station sometimes accepted volunteers, people to help out and set things up, clean the studio and make sure everything was running smoothly for the presenters.
This was too good an opportunity to miss, so when they said yes to him, he made sure that he was there whenever they needed him.

Pretty soon, people at the station started to notice him. He was the kid with hustle. The kid who knew his stuff. And most importantly, Frisky was the kid who was passionate about what he wanted to do.

It was the end of a long week, one in which he'd been at school all day and at the station every evening, just managing to finish his homework in the moments in between.
Frisky was just putting on his backpack, getting ready to leave, when someone called his name.

The guy didn't work there, but Frisky recognised him straight away.

He was the director of his favourite radio station. He'd been visiting and had noticed Frisky's hard work. He offered to mentor Frisky right there, on the spot.

This was it, Frisky thought. It was happening!
He said yes without a moment's hesitation and, over the next few weeks, couldn't believe the amount he was learning.
He was working with a real, professional radio DJ.
He was living the dream.

RADIO STATION

And not only that, but the director was impressed.
He'd never seen a kid that was so enthusiastic and, when the time was right, he knew that he'd have to give Frisky a chance.
But little did either of them know, that chance was just around the corner...

"Frisky!" the director said, as he walked in one evening. "I've got a question for you. A slot has just opened up on our overnight shift. How about you host your own show?" Frisky stared at him, his mouth open wide.
"Me?"

Once he'd calmed down, he shook the director's hand and took his seat in the studio the very next night.
It felt like home.
And for the next two years, it was.

It wasn't the best slot on the schedule, but Frisky loved it.
He had an audience listening to him, enjoying his music.
He had a following. He had fans!
And more importantly, he had confidence!
Frisky DJ was here, and there was no looking back.

After a while, the station knew that Frisky DJ couldn't stay on the night shift forever.
In fact, they knew where he'd be suited. He was energetic, passionate and...
Perfect for the morning slot!

His night-shift audience still listened to him, of course, and now so many others could as well. Everyone that had ever doubted him now listened to his show every day. Not that Frisky minded. He didn't need any sort of apology. After all, he just wanted to play some good music!

As the years went on, he couldn't believe that it had happened the way it had.
He was a DJ. He was DJing on stage for artists he loved. He was playing music and the people LOVED IT!
Every time he went into the studio, he remembered the journey he'd taken to get there and it made him smile.